Organization Design:

Reorganize Your Department or Company To Improve Performance

Step-By-Step

By
Cedric Ng Mong Shen

Copyright Cedric Ng Mong Shen 2020

Table of Contents

1) Introduction

2) Signs that it is time to reorganize your Department or Company

   2.1) Change in Strategy

   2.2) Problems in Company or Department

   2.3) Resignation of Personnel

3) Organizational Design Steps (Define Criteria, Diagnose Issues, Design Structure, Deliver Structure)

   3.1) Step 1 – Define Criteria

   3.2) Step 2 – Diagnose Issues

      3.2.1) Strategy

      3.2.2) Structure

      3.2.3) Process

      3.2.4) Rewards

      3.2.5) People

      3.2.6) Culture

      3.2.7) Environment

   3.3) Step 3 – Design Structure

      3.3.1) Size of company

      3.3.2) Levels and Span of control

      3.3.3) Grouping options

   3.4) Step 4 – Deliver Structure

3.4.1) Decide on the structure:

3.4.2) Transition to the structure:

4) Conclusion

Other Publications by the Author

1) Introduction

Organizations must be able to adapt their structures to capture new markets and expand existing ones. However, when Companies are not structured properly, business opportunities fizzle due to lack of attention, and turf wars stifle teamwork because of unclear responsibilities. Often Performance issues are a Structural issue rather than a Person issue. A company can have great people, great leadership and still not perform well because of poor organizational design.

Organization Design is more than moving the boxes. It is about how to configure your Department or Company structure to improve performance, and can be applied by Department managers at all levels. Organization Design work sometimes encompasses redesign of an entire company, but mostly the focus is at departmental level.

This book highlights the warning signs when organization design is needed, and provides a simple four-step framework to guide managers how to design effective Departments and Organizations:
- Step 1 – <u>Define</u> Criteria
- Step 2 – <u>Diagnose</u> Issues
- Step 3 – <u>Design</u> Structure
- Step 4 – <u>Deliver</u> Structure

Organizational Design steps			
Define Criteria	Diagnose Issues	Design Structure	Deliver Structure
Step 1 Define Scope of organization design, Issues to fix, Opportunities to tap	**Step 2** Diagnose Organizational Effectiveness using six dimensions (strategy, design, process, rewards, people, & culture)	**Step 3** Develop Structure Options, and Evaluate using defined criteria.	**Step 4** Decide on structure and Transition to it

2) Signs that it is time to reorganize your Department or Company

Existing Organization Structures lose relevance as market conditions change, or leadership change.

Signs that indicates it's time to reorganize your Department or Company structure include:
- Change in strategy
- Problems in Company or Department
- Resignation

2.1) Change in Strategy

Strategy cannot be successfully executed without the right organization design. When the Strategy changes, the structure needs to be redesigned to support it.

These are some examples of strategy changes that requires changes to structure:
- Change in market segmentation
- Change in company or department objectives
- Startup of a new business
- Shift from domestic to regional
- Mergers and Acquisitions

2.2) Problems in Company or Department

Problems in a department or company usually indicates the need to reorganize your Department or Company structure.

Some warning signs that call for an organizational redesign include:
- Conflicts between departments
- Employees complain that they are overloaded or underworked
- Employees complain that their work overlap
- Employees complain about communications breakdown
- Company, Department or Employee not meeting objectives
- High employee turnover
- Problems in cross-selling products and services to customers.
- Difficulty obtaining information and resources across departments
- Lengthy decision-making process

If these breakdowns are preventing the organization from executing its strategy or achieving its business goals, redrawing department boundaries is needed.

2.3) Resignation of Personnel

When a key employee leaves, don't assume that you must instantly replace them. Take the opportunity to question the existing structure and whether the role is necessary. Evaluate the requirements of the role, comparing them against the current employees' capabilities and career aspirations, and then review how the role should be redefined, who should fill it, and when. It's better to make the right decision than a fast decision.

3) Organizational Design Steps (Define Criteria, Diagnose Issues, Design Structure, Deliver Structure)

Organizational design decisions are inevitably complex and tweaking one area may produce unanticipated consequences in another area. However, the structure should be revisited when there are key changes in organization size, function/segment performance, leadership, legislations, and technology. To get the best Organizational design, we need to take the broad view, working step-by-step through the myriad tradeoffs. There are four main steps for Organizational Design:
- Step 1 – Define Criteria
- Step 2 – Diagnose Issues
- Step 3 – Design Structure
- Step 4 – Deliver Structure

Organizational Design steps			
Define Criteria	Diagnose Issues	Design Structure	Deliver Structure
Step 1 Define Scope of organization design, Issues to fix, Opportunities to tap	Step 2 Diagnose Organizational Effectiveness using six dimensions (strategy, design, process, rewards, people, & culture)	Step 3 Develop Structure Options, and Evaluate using defined criteria.	Step 4 Decide on structure and Transition to it

3.1) Step 1 – Define Criteria

Firstly, the organizational design team must get the stakeholders to agree on the design criteria early, as it will help guide the design and evaluation of the draft organization design models. Then use these criteria to evaluate the organizational design alternatives and to measure your success.

Examples of design criteria are:
- Scope of organization design
- Issues to fix
- Opportunities to tap

3.2) Step 2 – Diagnose Issues

After defining the design criteria, diagnose the effectiveness of the organizational effectiveness using seven dimensions (strategy, design, process, rewards, people, culture, and environment):

3.2.1) Strategy

Strategy is about how the company differentiates itself from its competitors in terms of market, products, pricing, or people. Organizational structures need to be aligned with changes in strategy, as it impacts the organization's ability to capture new markets and expand existing ones.

Diagnose the effectiveness of the current strategy with these questions:

- How does the company differentiate itself from its competitors in terms of market, products, pricing, or people? Do you think it is effective?

- What strategic opportunities do you see opening up for the company?

- Does your organization structure direct sufficient management attention to your sources of competitive advantage?

- Does your structure direct enough attention to each market segment or initiative. If no unit has responsibility for a segment or initiative, the design is probably flawed.

3.2.2) Structure

Often Performance issues are a Structural issue rather than a Person issue. A company can have great people, great leadership and still not perform well because of poor structure.

Diagnose the effectiveness of the current department or company structure with these questions:

- How does your structure make it easier or more difficult to achieve your strategy?

- Does your department's structure support the strategy?

- Which roles within your business unit do not align with your strategy or seem redundant?

- Which functions, teams, or roles do you need to create or eliminate to support the strategy?

- Identifying redundant-hierarchy can provide powerful insights on where an organization can cut management layers to add greater value. The basic organization design principle is to decentralize decisions to frontline units and retaining decisions at upper levels only if those levels can add value. If a level's propositions echo those of the level above or below it, one of the levels may be redundant.

3.2.3) Process

Disconnects in key processes across departments also signal a need for redesign. For example, Lengthy, cumbersome decision-making processes. The more similar work processes are across a company's units, the easier an employee can assimilate into a new position in a different operating unit and focus on learning what is different.

Diagnose the effectiveness of the company's key processes with these questions:

- Which departments do you need to collaborate with the most?

- Where do you have breakdowns in collaboration?

- Which processes support the achievement of your strategy, and which does not?

- Which processes are overly cumbersome, difficult to execute, and/or the most time consuming? Why?

- What impedes, or gets in the way of, accomplishing your goals?

- What new processes are needed?

3.2.4) Rewards

Rewards refers to salaries, promotions, bonuses, profit sharing, stock options, sales incentives, and so forth. The purpose of Rewards is to align the goals of the employee with the goals of the organization. Rewards must be congruent with the structure to influence the strategic direction.

Diagnose the effectiveness of the company's Rewards with these questions:

- What is currently working well, and what is not working well, to drive performance towards business unit goals?

- Are there opportunities to create new Reward and Recognition programs specific to your business unit?

- Do you feel that the company is rewarding and recognizing the right outcomes and behaviors with the right reward?

3.2.5) People

Does your design reflect the strengths, weaknesses, and motivations of your people? When a company has talented people that they want to retain, they play with the structure to create promotion opportunities for these people. Managers must make choices about how to group people together to perform their work, based on their employee's capability and preferences.

Diagnose the effectiveness of the company's People with these questions:

- Does the current talent capabilities support your department or company strategy?

- What new leadership capabilities are required that do not exist in your department or company?

- What talent capabilities need to be built, reduced, eliminated, or changed to succeed in the future?

- Do you know of any individuals who are not being utilized to their fullest potential, can be challenged to contribute more, or may be ready for new or larger opportunities?

3.2.6) Culture

Culture influences how work gets done, affects project success or failure, and says who fits in and who doesn't. Cultural issues may be responsible for low morale, absenteeism or high staff turnover. Sometimes, Culture is a more powerful way of managing employee behaviors than organizational rules. When a company is trying to improve the quality of its customer service, creating more customer service policies may not be as effective.

Diagnose the effectiveness of the company's Culture with these questions:

- Is your business unit culture aligned with the mission?

- When a problem is encountered, what rules do people apply when they solve it?

- Do employees get rewarded for good work or penalized for poor work?

- What daily behavior and actions of the people signal acceptable behavior?

- Which culture are detrimental to the health and productivity of the workforce?

- What culture does the firm want to encourage? Which culture is hindering the firm's strategy?

- What stories do people currently tell about the organization?

- Are there departments that need a distinct culture from the rest of the company?

3.2.7) Environment

The organization structure is also affected by external environment factors such as government regulations and technological changes. The company has to plan the organizational structure in accordance with the rules and policies of the country.

Understand the current and future company's external environment with this question:

- What are the biggest external challenges changes facing your department or company in the next one to three years? What is your department or company doing to respond to these challenges?

- Do government regulations in the country require the setting up of joint-venture with a local partner?

- If your company plans to move from country structure to Product structure, is your company's information systems able to report performance by product?

3.3) Step 3 – Design Structure

In step three, develop a few structure options and rank them against your design criteria. Remember, no option is perfect as there are always trade-offs. Pick the best one and come up with a plan to mitigate the risks.

When designing the Department or Company structure, consider these factors:

- **Size of company** - Companies of different sizes require different types of structure.

- **Levels and Span of control** - Optimum span of control depends on Organization size, Nature of organization, Nature of job, Skills and competencies of manager, Employees skills and abilities, Type of interaction between supervisors and employees, and tenure of manager

- **Grouping options** - Organizational structures can be grouped by function, product, customer, geographic, or process.

3.3.1) Size of company

Companies of different sizes require different types of structure. The design that works during start-up is different from what works during growth, maturity, and decline. Some organizations group start-ups together since start-ups face similar technical and commercial concerns and thus can share learning. Some organizations group start-ups, growth, mature and decline stages together so that start-ups can gain from the more experienced countries. Which route is chosen is a design decision that should be based on explicitly articulated rationale and clear criteria, and it should be revisited when the business life cycle changes and when the political and competitive environment changes.

- **Start-up**:

    New start-up usually have limited capital, thus they start small and use either use **selling partners** or hire their own **generalist sales forces**. Start-ups need a lot of effort to create brand awareness before sales can be generated.

- **Growth**:

    At growth stage, it's difficult for generalists sales force to sell the entire product line to multiple products and markets. Thus, Companies need to set up **specialist sales forces** that focus on products, markets, customer segments, or activities such as acquiring customers (hunters) or servicing existing customers (farmers). Every kind of specialization has pro and con. Many companies therefore create hybrid structures that include a mix of generalist as well as market, product, customer and activity specialist. As repeat sales become a larger proportion of sales, customers will require service and support. **Account managers** can be used to focus on all the needs of its major customers, while product specialists call on midsize clients that don't generate sufficient business to warrant account managers, and generalist salespeople cover small companies whose small accounts don't justify visits by several product specialist.

- **Maturity**:

    When businesses hit maturity, the emphasis shift to making sales forces more effective by appointing account managers, for the largest accounts and improving cost-efficiency by using less expensive **telesales staff** and **sales assistants**. Account managers coordinate the sales effort and bring in product specialists when deep expertise is needed. Sales assistants and **part-time salespeople** are deployed to woo small or geographically dispersed customers and to sell easy-to-understand products. Telesales staff is used to perform activities that don't need face-to-face contact with customers.

- **Decline**:

    When turnaround is unlikely and decline is inevitable, organizations **reduce the size of sales forces** and use even more cost-efficient ways to cover markets. Businesses at the decline stage use their salespeople to service the most profitable and strategically important customers. By using less-expensive selling resources, companies can continue selling to some segments. That entails moving the coverage of some customers **from specialty salespeople to generalist**, and shifting the coverage of other customers from field salespeople to telesales staff, shifting the selling of easy-to-understand products and administrative tasks to sales assistants, **telesales staff, part-time salespeople, and the internet.**

3.3.2) Levels and Span of control

Optimum span of control depends on Organization size, Nature of organization, Nature of job, Experience of manager, Experience of Employee, Type of interaction between supervisors and employees, and tenure of manager:

- **Organization size**:

    Larger organizations tend to have wider spans of control than smaller organizations.

- **Nature of organization:**

    Culture influences span of control. A more relaxed, flexible culture goes with wider span of control; whereas a hierarchical culture goes with narrow span of control.

- **Nature of job:**

    Routine and low complexity jobs require less supervision than complicated jobs. Have a wider span of control for jobs requiring less supervision, and a narrower span of control for more complex and vague jobs.

- **Experience of manager:**

    More experienced managers generally have wider spans of control than less experienced managers.

- **Experience of employee:**

    Less experienced employees require more guidance (closer supervision, narrow span of control); Whereas more experienced employees require less guidance (less supervision, wider span of control).

- **Type of interaction between supervisors and employees:**

    More frequent interaction goes with narrower span of control. Less interaction, such as supervisors just helping solve employee problems goes with wider span of control.

- **Tenure:**

    New Managers typically take on a broader array of responsibilities initially, as they need to understand the business. But once they know the business, they gradually reduce their span of control until the number of reports approaches the old norm.

3.3.3) Grouping options

Organizational structures can be grouped by function, product, customer, geographic, or process:

3.3.3.1) Geographical structure

The geographic structure works best for a single business or business with one set of closely related products. The more a product or service must be consumed near to where it is produced, or the more costly it is to move a product from its site of production, the more the organization should be organized by geography. Advances in telecommunications have made services such as retailing, baking, and education less constrained by production and transportation challenges, thereby giving increasingly less importance to grouping by geography.

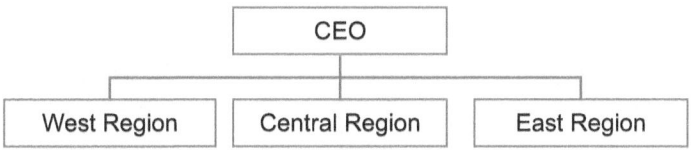

3.3.3.2) Product structure

The more the products can be standardized with little customization for local tastes, the more they can be managed on a global level, increasing the importance of the business grouping or product grouping over the geographic grouping. For example, Luxury goods are managed globally because brand consistency and image are primarily what is being sold.

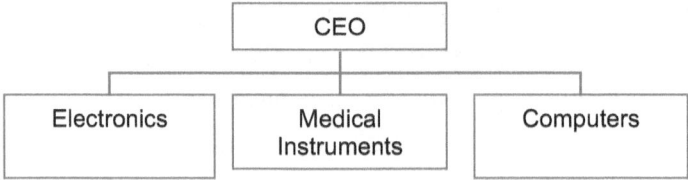

3.3.3.3) Market structure

In a Market structure, the organization is grouped by customer or industry. The advantages of Market structures, is that the company knows the needs of their customers better and can build stronger relationships with them.

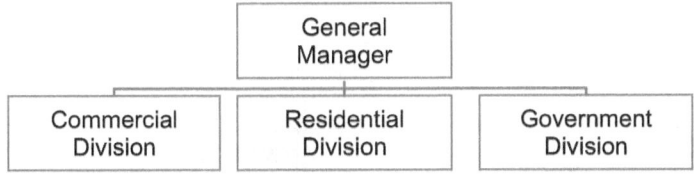

3.3.3.4) Process structure

When each process requires different skills, the process grouping works best because process grouping allows homogenous activities to be categorized (e.g. sawing, assembling, lacquering, etc).

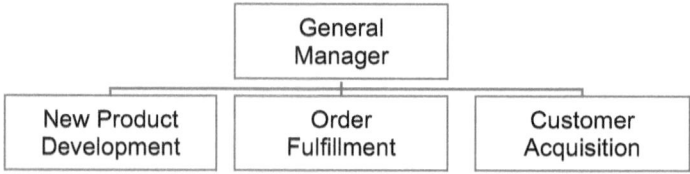

3.3.3.5) Functional structure

Functional structures put together people with common skills, knowledge, and orientations. This structure is cost efficient and allow in-depth specialization. There are likely common raw material requirements across the three product families. Commodity buying teams that cut across the three business units can identify common procurement items and negotiate better terms than segregating procurement within each business unit.

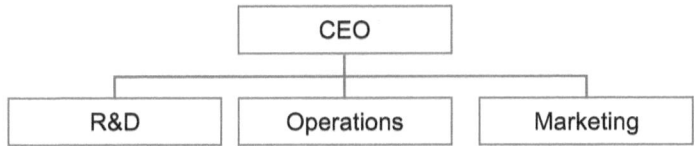

3.3.3.6) Multi Divisional structure

Owing to the complexity of tasks and the competitive environment in which organizations operate, firms often use a combination of the above-mentioned methods in departmentalization. E.g. an organization can put customer grouping as its primary organizing dimension, with product grouping as secondary, and geography grouping as third organizing dimension.

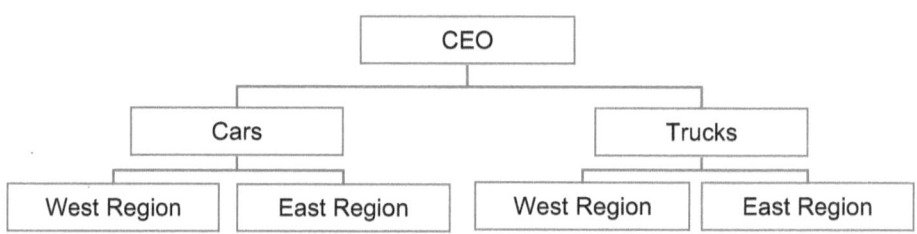

3.4) *Step 4* – *Deliver Structure*

In this step, we implement the new organizational structure (e.g. Communicate new structure, and train people in new roles/skills).

3.4.1) Decide on the structure:

Weigh the benefits of each structure and determine whether the design supports the firm's key sources of advantage (speedy introduction of products, low cost manufacturing, etc). Maintaining a divisional structure requires that each division operates as an independent business unit and cost center resulting in higher operational costs compared to a centralized functional structure. Although the product/customer structure offers more flexibility than the functional structure, it does not offer the level of operational control, and the matrix offers the benefits of both.

3.4.2) Transition to the structure:

Implementing the Organizational Design is as challenging as creating it. The organization design team should provide a step-by-step plan for making the transition between current and future organizational models. Examples of transition plan includes, redeploying employees, training employees for their new roles in the new structure, out-placing separated employee, and keeping key people engaged so they can retain essential talent through the transition.

Every organization design must have a balance between what is good for a company in theory and what is possible (political realities). Powerful individuals can sabotage the execution of the organization design. Determine which losers are influential and formulate a strategy to deal with them - either buying their support through enhanced compensation packages or neutralize their influence by changing their roles or letting them go.

4) Conclusion

Organizational design decisions are inevitably complex, and tweaking one area may produce unanticipated consequences in another area. To get the best design, you need to take the broad view, working step-by-step through the myriad tradeoffs. The faster the design can be aligned, the faster the CEOs can turn the ship and sail it to "the promised land".

Other Publications by the Author

https://www.amazon.com/Designing-Global-Sales-Incentive-Plans-ebook/dp/B07FW14LFZ/ref=sr_1_7?keywords=cedric+ng+mong+shen&qid=1553281332&s=books&sr=1-7

Your company has hundreds of patchwork sales incentive plans developed by various business units after decades of mergers & acquisitions. Sales incentive plans for B2C sales is not effective to drive performance for B2B sales, and frequently individual sales quotas are not set properly. As the Global Rewards Director, you are assigned by your CEO to reduce the number of sales incentive plans and align it to corporate strategy. Do you know what to do?

The key to designing an effective global sales-compensation framework is to identify performance measures and design principles that can apply globally and yet provide some flexibility for business unit or local customization. This book teaches you a nine step, 3D6P approach to design effective global sales incentive plans (Diagnose the root cause of poor sales, Determine change management strategy, Determine eligibility, Pay strategy, Performance measures, Plan mechanics, Payout scenario, Plan documentation & communication, Plan effectiveness). The concepts and examples in this book, works for all companies of all sizes, in all industries. The concept is comprehensive and yet flexible. Companies can choose to use all or parts of the steps to design their sales incentive plan.

https://www.amazon.com/Designing-Salary-Structures-Step-Step-ebook/dp/B07G264J11/ref=sr_1_3?keywords=cedric+ng+mong+shen&qid=1553280240&s=books&sr=1-3

Your CEO returned from a management retreat with a new strategic business plan that will revitalize the company and lead it into lucrative new markets. As the Director of Compensation and Benefits, you are charged with translating the strategic business plan into a pay strategy that supports the company's vision and business strategy. Do you know what to do?

To design the Salary structures that drive business results and performance, you need to know which positions are "hot skills", which positions are difficult-to-hire, which positions have high attrition rate, and which functions are strategic functions. Each of these has implications for designing a salary structure that drives business results and performance. Salary structures provide guidelines for making pay related decisions within an organization, bridging the gap between where you are today and where you want to be tomorrow (target pay positioning). This book shows you in six simplified steps, how to design strategic salary structures:
1) Establish your pay positioning.
2) Establish job worth hierarchy.
3) Develop job grades.
4) Develop pay range.
5) Calculate structural parameters (pay range, min, max).
6) "Slot" your employees and tweak your salary structure.

https://www.amazon.com/Reviewing-Employee-Benefits-using-model-ebook/dp/B07FXSYKB2/ref=sr_1_3?keywords=cedric+ng+mong+shen&qid=1553017293&s=books&sr=1-3

Your CEO returned from a management retreat with a new strategic business plan that will revitalize the company and lead it into lucrative new markets. As the Global Rewards Director, you are tasked with designing a "Global Benefits Philosophy & Strategy" that can be applied across different business units and countries. --- Do you know what to do?

Do you have difficulty getting Union buy-in to reduce employee benefits? Do you have difficulty convincing your CEO to enhance employee benefits? Do you have difficulty explaining why company can't give employees cash allowances instead of benefits?

This book addresses all these issues and provides a framework to help you to formulate your company's global employee benefits positioning and strategy. Employee Benefits reflect the culture of the organization and differentiate its Employer brand. A company without differentiated Benefits Strategy is like a ship that follows where the wind blows without any direction of its own.

https://www.amazon.com/Predictive-HR-Analytics-Mong-Shen-ebook/dp/B07KWZ86DK/ref=sr_1_1?keywords=cedric+ng+mong+shen&qid=1553279368&s=books&sr=1-1

Most people struggle with analytics because they don't have a structured framework to an unstructured problem. Predictive analytics helps you see what is invisible to others, so you know which behaviors differentiate your most successful employees, creating a competitive advantage over those that rely on gut feel. This book explains how to use the structured five-step ARHAT approach for Predictive HR Analytics (Ask Questions, Review Literature, Hypothesis Formulation, Analyze Data, Tell the Story). Numerous real-world examples are included, which will be useful in your hypothesis formulation (i.e. If X and Y is done, then Z will happen). Most books just discuss about HR analytics without showing you how to run statistical analysis. This book not only discuss about HR analytics, but teaches you data-storytelling and data-visualization techniques, and statistical techniques such as Decision trees, Correlation, Multiple Regression, Chi-Square, and R programming. It covers the entire scope of Predictive HR Analytics (Benefits, Compensation, Culture, Diversity & Inclusion, Engagement, Leadership, Learning and Development, Personality Traits, Recruitment, Sales Incentives), and shows you how Predictive HR Analytics can be used to answer questions such as:

(1) Predict who are the people at risk of leaving.
(2) Identify where the best people come from and how successful a candidate will be if hired.
(3) Predict impact of employee engagement on customer satisfaction, revenue and Shareholder Returns.
(4) Predict financial impact of training.
(5) Predict Diversity & Inclusion's impact on revenue.
(6) Predict employee absenteeism and accident.

https://www.amazon.com/dp/B07PXRLL3Z/ref=sr_1_5?keywords=cedric+ng+mong+shen&qid=1553272657&s=books&sr=1-5

You don't need to buy expensive statistical software like SPSS. This book teaches you R (R can be downloaded for free), People Analytics, Social Media Analytics, Text Mining and Sentiment Analysis. It is written for people with no knowledge of R, with step-by-step print-screen instructions. You don't need Statistical knowledge, as R executes the statistical number crunching (Correlation, Multiple & Logistic Regression, etc.) for you, by simply entering a few commands. This book covers the full People Analytics scope (Benefits, Compensation, Culture, Diversity & Inclusion, Engagement, Leadership, Learning & Development, Personality Traits, Performance Management, Recruitment, Sales Incentives) with numerous real-world examples, and shows how **R** can help you:

1) Run Social Media Analytics, Text mining & Sentiment Analysis with R.
2) Predict employees' flight-risk using R's Correlation & Logistic Regression function.
3) Identify the personality traits of top performing Customer Service staff and Sales staff using R's correlation function.
4) Predict impact of Employee Engagement on Customer Satisfaction, Revenue and Shareholder Returns, etc. using R's Correlation & Multiple Regression function.
5) Predict impact of Learning & Development on Sales, using R's Multiple Regression function.
6) Predict Diversity & Inclusion's impact on Revenue and EBIT using R's Multiple Regression function.

https://www.amazon.com/dp/B07TW7V7F5/ref=sr_1_2?keywords=ng+mong+shen&qid=1562036969&s=books&sr=1-2

A lot of organizational data is often untapped unstructured data in the form of text & numbers. For those who don't want to spend months learning R programming & for those who can't afford to buy expensive SPSS statistical software. This is the only book that teaches you how to use Microsoft Excel for Predictive HR Analytics, Text Mining & Organizational Network Analysis (ONA) with step-by-step print-screen instructions:

1) Predictive HR Analytics: Use Excel's Statistical Analysis tools (Decision trees, Correlation, Multiple & Logistic Regression) to run Predictive HR Analytics. E.g. an employee is predicted to have a 60% probability of getting into accidents, if he is age 25, worked 1 year in the company & took 6 days sick leave. An employee is predicted to get rated "7" for Customer Service, if the training program that he attended has a training evaluation score of "8". An employee is predicted to resign if she is age 23, worked for 2 years, and takes 60 minutes to commute to work.

2) Organizational Network Analysis (ONA): Run ONA using Excel's network analysis tool. Learn how to convert an employee's organizational network into a score & then predict if they will be a high-potential (HiPo). E.g. an employee is predicted to be a HiPo with performance rating of "9", if his "Social Network Size" is "16", "Social Network Diversity Index" is "3" & "Competency Score" is "8".

3) Text Mining, Sentiment Analysis & Word Clouds: Mine text from social network posts, employee engagement surveys & Glassdoor comments, then run Sentiment Analysis using Excel & visualize the insights with "Word Clouds". Learn how to predict a company's average employee attrition rate based on its sentiment. E.g. a company's average employee attrition rate is predicted to be 8%, if unemployment rate is 3%, GDP growth is 2%, Glassdoor public sentiment rating is "5", and engagement score is "7".

https://www.amazon.com/dp/B0859CB567/ref=sr_1_2?keywords=ng+mong+shen&qid=1582910007&s=books&sr=1-2

The 21st century is redefined by a data-driven revolution & gig economy. But, to date, employee engagement has not been based on a data-driven model. This makes it difficult to justify investment in employee engagement programs with the rigor that a data-driven CEO expects. IISS is the 1st & only book that incorporates Employee Experience & Engagement with Predictive Analytics. It offers a fresh way to cultivate engagement using "4 Engagement Bags" & "5 Engagement Fertilizers".

Bag 1) Inspire with Engagement Investment: Inspire with Predictive Analytics, and Inspire with Stories & Data Visualisation Techniques

Bag 2) Inspire with Engagement Fertilizers: Making employees happy, doesn't mean they will work hard for the organization. Use the 5 "Engagement Fertilizers" to build great employee experience & engagement:
- **Fertilizer 1: Basic Needs** – Soil, Rain, Sun
- **Fertilizer 2: Social Needs** – Birds
- **Fertilizer 3: Growth Needs** – Nutrients
- **Fertilizer 4: Meaning** – Healthy Tree
- **Fertilizer 5: Expectations** – Fruits!

Bag 3) Sentiment Gathering: Pulse Surveys, Focus Groups, Glassdoor Reviews, IISS Engagement Diagnosis Questions.

Bag 4) Sentiment Diagnosis & Prescription: Engagement Metrics & Dashboards, Bar Charts, Radar Charts, Word Clouds, Sentiment Analysis, Correlation, Regression, IISS Engagement Prescriptions.

www.ingramcontent.com/pod-product-compliance
Lightning Source LLC
Chambersburg PA
CBHW030518220526
45464CB00006B/2853